Charenton

Also by Chus Pato:

In Galician:
Urania. Vigo: Calpurnia, 1991.
Heloísa. A Coruña: Espiral Maior, 1994.
Fascinio. Muros: Toxosoutos, S.L., 1995.
A ponte das poldras. Santiago de Compostela: Noitarenga, S.C., 1996.
	(2nd edition: Galaxia, 2006).
Nínive. Vigo: Xerais, 1996.
Heloísa. Madrid: La Palma, 1998.
m-Talá. Vigo: Xerais, 2000.
Charenton. Vigo: Xerais, 2004.

In Galician and Spanish:
Un Ganges de palabras (selected poems edited and translated by Iris Cochón, Colección Puerta del mar, CEDMA, Málaga, 2003).

In English:
from m-Talá (chapbook trans. Erín Moure, Nomados, Vancouver, 2002)

Also by Erín Moure:

O Cadoiro
Little Theatres
O Cidadán
A Frame of the Book
Pillage Laud
Search Procedures
The Green Word: Selected Poems 1973-1992
Sheepish Beauty, Civilian Love
WSW (West South West)
Furious
Domestic Fuel
Wanted Alive
Empire, York Street

CHUS PATO

Charenton

translated by Erin Moure

Shearsman Books & BuschekBooks
Exeter   Ottawa

First published in the United Kingdom in 2007 by
Shearsman Books Ltd
58 Velwell Road
Exeter EX4 4LD   www.shearsman.com

ISBN 978-1-905700-33-2

and in Canada by
BuschekBooks
P O Box 74053
Ottawa, Ontario K1M 2H9   www.buschekbooks.com

ISBN 978-1-894543-44-6

Original text copyright © María Xesús Pato Díaz, 2004;
copyright © Edicións Xerais de Galicia, S.A., 2004.
Translations copyright © Erín Moure, 2007.

The right of Chus Pato, to be identified as the author, and Erín Moure to be identified as the translator of this work has been asserted by them in accordance with the Copyrights, Designs and Patents Act of 1988. All rights reserved. No part of this publication may be reproduced, stored in a retrieval system, transmitted in any form or by any means, electronic, mechanical, photocopying, recording or otherwise, without the prior permission of the publisher.

Library and Archives Canada Cataloguing in Publication

Pato, Chus, 1955-
    Charenton / Chus Pato; translated from the Galician by
    Erín Moure.

Poems.
Translation of the Galician book by the same title.
ISBN 978-1-894543-44-6 (BuschekBooks)
ISBN 978-1-905700-33-2 (Shearsman)

    I. Mouré, Erin, 1955- II. Title.

PQ9469.2.P37C4313 2007   869.15   C2007-904006-3

to Heriberto Bens

for such beauty to exist you have to imagine a wall [(– this wall, is it high?) (– vast)] of brick with buttresses shoring up its rhythm; in front of it, a green border masks a doorway lost in time. An older poet walks past here each morning, her emotions more or less / like the building, boarded up, abandoned to disintegrate. To her, doubts have the texture of gorges and the pent gasp of mouth-to-mouth, and as for her more or less – poetic? – efforts, she's not sure if she should keep dragging this code through narrow and twisting alpine passes, or if she should persevere or not with the taxing exercises of rescue and shipwreck, if she should just give up all that has been obsession and justification for life.

now she sets soft greenery in front of you (moss) that grows at the rim of sewer covers or in the geometrical quadrangles of flagstones (in fact, there's a sidewalk here). In the middle, the poet, devastated as an architecture (without acanthus, capital, fust, doric) – possibly even the building at 15, B Street in the strangest of towns, in a remote country – was stopped short by a disappearance, by lack of energy, of projects... by the corrosion of years. Later a first field of frost.

the dream is of a remote bombardment. tree roots overgrow the city's destruction,
it dreams (the tree) this bombardment, remote in time

neither sap nor squirrel grasp what i know: that the forest flourishes over the rubble of a decimated city

as the tree dreams, so does a heart: in Baghdad-Vietnam, in shell-pocked Afghan ranges, on the coasts of Galicia, in Hiroshima

i'd point out the highest number of dead, but where does it
end? *the heart of a century,* when did it start to form?
and how and where

it's something of unusual value
in the ample vestibule of the place where i work // it's
stone

no one, not even the best ballerina, can cross the laser barrier
that protects it
not even the most agile girl-contortionist of Tonking or
ancient China

it's granite
you can see it if you look close to the edge where it's laminated
but never through the mantle that coats it
a mantle that writes the century's root, there where the heart
splits into two breasts or two hills

oilTactile, supremacist

---

from the immense perhercynicalian stones (discontinuous
from Malpica to Tui) out to salicornian coral

loop

the body folds inward to become lake, in the trance hundreds of faces of the child buddha, in procession, filed through the bedroom

**though it's not far, someone (male) under the arcades of the Main Square insists on accompanying me. We move at extreme speed veering past all sorts of obstacles (Mumbai, Calcutta, in any case through a non-Western city). We return to the starting point

it acts as a metaphor for poetic labour, the rhapsodist occupies the copilot's seat (no one drives the automobile), the mathematical muse is in the back, protected from the wind by the trunk lid, she propels the vehicle

dreams leave no contiguous mark on the immediate desire of the body an imposing square, abrupt (hemmed in by buildings, medieval or napoleonic), points the way to this main floor where we won't find sarcophagi, just a meticulous and monotonous succession of hyperboreal columns and chaldean arches

a lacunal sky, a bog or basin, metaphorical and elusive, covers this frontspiece of love (or codex) in which it is possible to intuit necromantic facades and towers, along with nuptial flowers and leonine butterflies in that purest Venetian style which a brilliant native bard calls an Amazonia of granite

it sweeps upward in a vertical of igneous intrusion
its pages are of fog, thick fog or smoke, dense smoke
they're born from heat concentrated in the air above the earth's frigidity or from the combustion of oaks, right where their trunks are most vulnerable to destruction by stag beetles. All in all, it's clearer than the night that surrounds it (a thousand ewes and Karakoul rams), Chernozen, black

a heart centred, a ramification of arteries (...)

1

when i affirm
"they, my ancestors, had a home (idiom, territory), knew vocables to describe any /all accident of topography"
and i maintain
"i don't live on the earth as my ancestors did, i don't know any names (idiom-territory) other than forest, tree, field of grain"
i'm not making a value judgement, i don't set myself up in opposition nor do i consider myself a subject of progress
i say
"they were labourers, tied to the triennial rotation of crops and before that to the glebe"
i note a discharge of power, a paradigm shift

⋆⋆

to codify emigration not simply as an assault on identity [(of we Galicians) as a people] but also as a negation and search for freedom (resistance against horrific working conditions and freedom of new political conditions, conditions of life)

[on the desire for mobility]

2

explore the following discourses:
the mercantile argument of the modern age, the romantic
subject of the first industrial revolution // the poem-machine
of the avant-gardes (assembly line, taylorism)

value theory in the era of informational accumulation
decide which kinds of individuation and poetic bodies produce
and which scriptural prototypes block these propositions or are
fundamentalist (nostalgic-backwards)

which is to say, link production machines // gradients in the
poem

as this poem 'No Delicacies' by I. Bachmann did with the Cold
War at its point of highest tension

(...) i have learned meaning
with words
that exist
(for the lowest class)

hunger
       dishonour
              tears
                     darkness (...)

(Someone really should. Others should.)

My part, let it be lost.

and it's mind-boggling even by half because it's life and death and the here and now is the south seas

canterbury-bells clamped shut in awesome sheaths of masculine protection; so there'll be blossoms, if they snow over the dunes, water not quite hardened

my feet do it automatically, clench at the cliff-face like a colony of goose-barnacles

**

(...) on the other hand i persisted in seeing the reeds in imagist fashion and approached blackened sands and whiter sands, dunes and dune grasses, discerned congers seabass and black-bellied anglers out of the great ocean waters... such obsessed description... i also feel incredible *reserves of fear*, of bivalves and crustaceans//of sheer prodigiousness

under a pretentious awning (precarious); musicians from the steppes, here from the far ends of the globe, played lutes, wind instruments, portentious keyboards and endless percussion and above it all, an ecstatic voice... i couldn't drag myself away from the tent before three, four, five in the morning
now the mountain range is etched in stony clarity, lily light, rosy sea-light, begins to recede as do the songs, but the cerebral spinning of the earth or forests hadn't yet begun, the warren of the deeps hadn't yet touched me... Jekyll hadn't left me either, in the intoxication of his singular present he talks endlessly to me under matted August vines tangled up and invaded by night's *dark lightning*. Jekyll (my little-death/petite-a in the symbolic house of language, dissection department, studies in anatomy)

i check on the children napping in their lairs (stuck to the mossy roots: a small sun, east)

i am the pyramid of Cheops, the temple of Hatshepsut and as beautiful as Attila
my heart

an exodus from Earth

the vending machine for language-intelligence can push its own button. Submerged plants tremble (Barbizon school) in the force of the river. Where batrachia / once thrived

literally, huge deactivated machines fertilize my CsO

my memories **don't want immortality**

i never listened to Sara-nat, didn't see her / ever. i'm Sara-nat when rain fills my lungs (the text). And – such pleasure! – the void

a heart is an infinite of language

inside, it cardio-propels itself [(40-400 stenosphere) crust] like a drift of continents i don't know how it will all end and i don't care either but i think maybe i should look for the final vertex that might lead me to a different azimuthal projection or Mercator mapping

(the opaque black membrane)

a good part of this book *Charenton* was written by Liberty Aguirre (...) the author knows little of her; i know she works with mirrors (she runs a small hydraulics and dredging firm that cleans and maintains locks, canals and rivers). She's an expert in Lacanian psychoanalysis; in fact, it was a sub-contract for dredging the Seine that brought her to this line of thought; visits to Charenton and Saint Anne, where she finds or found interned her most respected acquaintances, led her to study this therapy or method of psychological cure

the author worries about L's health, her recent departure to the ruins of Wadi Halfa where she decided to coordinate, despite her advanced years, site work to make new excavations possible, her unwavering insistence on looking for Franziska Ranner whom we all know disappeared... in such strange and painful circumstances (perhaps a cerebral trauma, consequence of the powerful and insensate blows self-inflicted against the stones of the pyramids after the horror of successive interviews with Doctor Körner in Cairo, from whom she received no extermination "you sire were in Dachau and in... in... Hartheim. Today i remember..."), suddenly disappeared, as we were saying, after the Aswan High Dam inundated that remote city

the last news from her was disturbing, a card from Alexandria: "EGYPTIAN DARKNESS, AFTER ALL, IS ABSOLUTE."[1]

---

[1] Ingeborg Bachmann, *The Book of Franza*

shoes are an object from my interior... for Antón Lopo

the carnivalesque snippet *dialogue between the muse and the soul*, for Emilio Araúxo

for such beauty to exist... for Miguel Casado

the discovery that Horda is a raft-island, on which human embryos are preserved

– madame do you share Jekyll's obsessions?
– Jekyll has no obsessions
– for all his constant talk of non-power, of not tuning in to the ancestral murmur, to the romantic-sublime animal, uncommonly blue, with the marks of the orthopedic corset that impede his movements
– sometimes Jekyll's state is confused
– he declaims his pain caused by the writing inscribed directly on his body, the hydraulic machines, the despotic signifiers, how would you say it, Mariana?
– Mariana tries to explain Jekyll... the abandoned tennis courts, gorgeous girls, hair blond and ardent in the haze of sunset, birds of Laguna Beach... this impossible evocation of the absolute; the office a surgical amphitheatre (full of chemical products, dissection implements)
– and the mastabas?
– they're ermine, graduated

(construction of an electronic barrier at the 17th parallel, attacks on Hanoi and Haiphong)

a bell sounds, the shipwrecked wash up on the sands

she's extracted from the mother as is a blood sample from inside our bodies but the analyst's technique is not exactly that of circulation of the blood

MULTITUDINOUS PROMETHEA: (enter, go to the spot where the orphic poet will later be) **while the skylark still learns pleasure, you think there's delight inside its song, an uncontrollable art the world wouldn't listen to you as you do the skylark**

in burrows as long as elephant trunks, in their dark calcineous earth, their green impending humidity

like the pale nocturnal fogs of my native cosmopolis (altitude marks, recesses in the poem that don't like to attract attention)

– and what's this supposed to mean: that to judge by the way i dress, i'm obviously from an Atlantic climate?

if only i knew English or some other foreign language (optional in this list of ways to reach perfection: the ability to water-ski)

to drive a Meteor, the exhaust-pipe… you realized but would never see it as problematic for thinking

a book weighs nothing, on a scale for weighing bodies, the
needle, its needling, is scarcely perceptible

,,,

    dream of Wittgensteinian landscape
    non-mother stone: writing

        300 metres in freefall
        volume: 3,475 km^2
        inner zone, radio: 1,255 km^2 (solid or crystalline)
        composition: (probable) iron, nickel
        temperature: 2,200-2,250° centigrade
        pressure: 3 or 4 million times that of the
        atmosphere at sea level
        sensation: entirely pleasant

i'm hegemonically alone in childhood (but with no gender identification or sexual marking). Yet i didn't have, radically, "no body"

,,,

(hermaphroditic fluency)

what's hard to imagine is not the appearance but the body of Heliogabalus K. (not a technical problem, just that H.K. hasn't the least possibility of existing.) And the cafe in which Iris K. and Heliogabalus K. run into each other, the freeway and service centres where vehicles cross paths, the room where i am (a site of highest but not the most rigorous security)

given that the art of poetry consists of making cyclopean stones lighter, such dolmens or cylinders of Santa Clara, grabbing them and even making them fly
she hurls objects against the heavens, not exactly uplifting but that let her hands defy gravity once more, to reach various asteroids

(...) what with the corrosion, the ascent was particularly difficult. Despite the sad state of my bronchials i was able to activate verticality while//effecting a wide opening in the ceiling of palm trees, i launched chunks of rusty roofstrut at my official persecutors, puttis out of any old 14thc Pompeyan fresco: baroque cherubim or cupids who tried insistently to hit me with splendid arrows

there's no lift; the edifice, built at the start of the 20th century in some native city of the author: Panama, near the Equator, the tropics what i'm trying to say is that this path which someone, already impossible to identify in this dimension, takes each morning or the registering of successive roman foundations, acts as or is taken as model for the various diggings, saturations or chemical strata of the novel, which definitely conceives of its topographical varieties as archaeological excavation or intoxication (narcotic)

like flowers, blooming from inside your eyes, the letters. You get up to see if you can shake them off: they stick. Cradle-transparency words. They suck you through tunnels of Green vegetation, flatlands that are not The Limia, patches of greenery you can't get through, ships. You treat them as if they were foreign vocables and spend hours peering into the Latin dictionary, into the anthology of French Literature, the sole ones you love. You decide on their meaning because to your mind such words are always interchangeable. You loathe these terms because you want to endure, because clover dodder doesn't exist, nor BRIARS, nor oaks. Thus *you spin round*, or it's the lay of the ground that changes direction. From this point on, words mark risks, of identity-character you all crossed the threshold to a position-café whose cellars were pool halls of masculine purity (in a suspension that produces poetry in me); shackled into the rock and angled: safety and alarm cables. Only one of you could transport my body. i descended, yes // to that infernal circle of incorruptible purity i laid out my clothes and when i woke it was raining; you have to realize rain here is a product of the condensation of the Styx, a fog that blurs any throw of the dice. i headed to my cubicle (it's something i do often: twice a year for 46 already) but this time i found it hard; not so much because i'd abandoned my home but because of the uncomfortable journey; i could go so far as to talk of a breakdown in the saurian lungs, or an anxiety attack... the equinoxes are a huge dragoness wrapping the axis of the earth, or imaginary line: rising in spring. i manage to keep the house functioning (kingdoms such as Dahomey, Zanzibar), washed the blinds, cooked and went for walks in an oak forest: i share nothing. The sky's radiant, perhaps i just wasn't able to shake off the muck that impedes thought. the workers start up at 8 a.m.: they excavate the earth then cover the hole with gravel, pour concrete (a rectangle). there's so much i don't experience in any city, a wall of elder bushes isolates me. the sameness is providential; the climate senseless. each day it's harder to work, i think this is paradise

it appears in front of you as the irruption of an alpine fold. All you can do is imagine the missing mountain profile and the root-crevice (right down to the incandescent nickel) of the cordillera

i write "horse": girls with women's bodies who play horse (not mare) because it implies to the male/males and to me that, inside and outside, we contemplate the male/males not just for those who flaunt themselves but, also and above all, this boy-male-stallion

we'd closed down the *Cheops*. Ruth stands on the top step of the stairwell that leads to a basement room where they might serve us breakfast; with her, young men almost adolescent compose a triangle of majesty (their tongues thick, sex splendid)
i think: Laocoön (Ruth is the snake coiled round the statue's young)
i think: Fassbinder (there are police all around us)

before her Ruth has what she calls "beauty"

---

thus the space must be that of the poem; in one place (basement dugout, hideaway or den) or another, the public square before dawn is pleasure; its canon is the body
what's left // (multiple series in frames) // of chaotic enumerations

shoes are an object from my interior, given i can see them at eye level// in flight, not just them but the brown fog that invades them
they're vermilion, spike-heeled

He walks diagonally across the stage, sits in the chair where a minute ago a worker lunched on a hamburger (silver paper), pulls off his own and with slight difficulty introduces his feet into the shoes
goes out and back, startles himself, walks
they're the shoes of Thetis, the sea goddess who birthed him; they keep on intoning
"i'll not give up the fruit of my womb, not to you, my lord! to death"

he retraces his steps diagonally, pulls off the shoes
– that's when i can see them, when i close my eyelids –
of blood, fire, ambrosia

---

                                                    life: tenuous

what you've just seen is night with its sanguine border, as any other grail predicts

add to this the idea of walking atop books, so that the paving stones are volumes (the path, millennia later, overgrown with grass and the root-*statumen* one metre deep
the navel of god lets loose a tornado or column that are all the texts in your womb in helicoidal Salomon

★★

this is Pamir, this is Nefertari (her body ruled by a multitude of ka(s) or doubles), this is a mirror (the birth of Venus, this birth of Venus lit up by the storm), this is Charenton, a sea-star in its Taiwanese purple ocean. It becomes impossible... a geode, a tiger, two portraits. The forest of Bethlehem

the first or outer circle Delphine Eydé marks by raking from the furthest point in; the second is us collecting the fruit; the third is a truncated cone of husks round the foot of the tree (thus frost can't mar the flavour of the chestnuts); the final is the branches that reach into the blue like a parasol of Antioch or awning over the carriage of Ashurbanipal
when he shoots at the powerful animal the colour of sand (female) or when sharpened sticks in the cartwheels mow down the life of the enemy

**

if i empty my mind the waters come, then the fortress, the bird (all that rises in the air) is root and the fish closest to the heavens

i doesn't coincide. The poem is not a privileged game of language

i don't know if i'm compatible or not with the forest

but also: *das kapital,* no more than a grain of sand in the tempest of the species and now the panopticon is a ruin

never mind for i can imagine the landscape however i want
if a desert, it'll be a tell
if rich with vegetation, wisteria will grow over the building
if in Antarctica, it'll be a phantasmagoria of ice

some folks (working women, crazies, schoolchildren, poets) still live there, they don't realize no one guards them

for in times of plenitude, systems of domination don't pay attention any more to populations, they don't have to feed them

just as you were saying, "capital is illiterate"

i have to get out:

exit biology, remain in my body

(2)

– is it true madam that you wish to be Moses?
– well, it's true that the possibility is open to me of leading my people across the Sinai
– are you aware of the desperation of your progenitor?
– i'm aware of the repression of his desire, in the end i wasn't thrown (baby stroller and all) off the New Bridge
– this saved you?
– rather, it saved my father; i'd have survived anyhow

– do you acknowledge your signature on this document, madam?
– i acknowledge being an avid reader of the pages of *Faust* (Adrian Leverkühn)
– did you ever sign a pact with the Devil?
– (...)

(1)

*

i get the order to run, so i run, **manage to reach the table**, sit down
(immediately surrounded by ladies) who, authoritarian, insist i get up; i explain, politely, that i'm saving the table for my mother and her friends, the ladies demand, i watch my mother's group approach slowly, languidly; the ladies start to threaten me, i don't relent, finally my mother's friends arrive, i smile courteously, the ladies // melt away

**

from that tower, the same thing always happens; two images one after the other

in one, the triremes of Caesar (exhausted from lack of money) arrive; they beat the ocean with their oars, frighten the natives, vanish

in the second there's nothing to be seen
but a heart, ecstatic as a shamrock, pulses: Ireland! Ireland!

****

he carefully folds the newspaper, says
– relax, we're on firm ground
then
"this city is an atoll governed by a crazed viceroy"

to open your eyes was to contemplate a garland of cigarette papers looped across the wall, on it, Antonin Artaud's face repeated to infinity

only an anarcho-mathematical muse could travel hundreds of kilometres, then bide her time till the author (she or he) deigns to assign her one, none (or all) of his-her-those //papers

Pleistocene: "the past is a far country" (m.o.)

AUTOBIOGRAPHY FOR TRUCHIS (written by herself)

girl-moses

to be extracted from the mother like a blood sample is from our insides (the name, fragile fluid of civilization). the technique applied by the analyst is not exactly that of the circulation of the blood

but my bones are not found in ontological opposition to my flesh
the acid earth of my mother-sonosphere obscenely devours my happy skeleton

    on pain and the apprehension of space

notwithstanding, it's useful, the "I" is, for example, for knowing what floor you're on without having to ask, for orienting yourself with a map ("I"-decipherer of codes) because individuals resemble persons but are institutions. The mother-territory contacts the daughter-territory to find out how we are; i answer we're fine, that you're going to have a hepatic extraction. If the mother-institution were a person i'd tell her your liver (i saw it) is full of stars, which isn't very precise, i should say "your hepatic cells are star-shaped"

it all happens so fast; the earth that wasn't the same, nor that of the hereafter–promise but a Florida, vanishes and the desert grows (under my feet, obviously)

i must produce earth. Earth manufactures itself from an precise position of the body in space. The poem can survive in the kingdom of snows

madam, is what you **write representative?**
- nothing represents, it produces
- it searches out meaning?
- nothing means, it functions

,,,

- does it have to do with a metaphysical language?
- no, with a transcendental language
- ideological?
- no, material
- oedipal?
- no, schizophrenic
- imaginary?
- no, it has nothing to do with an imaginary idiom, it's a non-figurative language
- symbolic?
- no, real
- structural?
- no, machinic
- molar, gregarious?
- no, molecular, micropsychic and micrological
- expressive?
- productive

the outside of the poem: its height, eye colour, the sex to which
it belongs; when
it eats, sleeps, walks
is it different than when we say: thought, i, consciousness?

does the poem have an inside / outside?

do all these words (intellect, mind, reason...) belong to the inside?

    is it private, the language the poet uses when configuring
    the inside of the poem?

is there an outside?

is it private?

        language is a labyrinth of pathways
        a traffic

*

an inner voice, we listen to this singular voice; we await orders, await instructions from this inner voice

but an internalized voice is made up of every written text, read by those eyes-voice, made up of all we've spoken, of all that is not verbal (audible)

we await orders; is this how we write?

we say *the poem is inspired*
we listen to the inner voice (the poet's)
we await orders, instructions from this incarcerated voice, so inspired, of the poet

we thank the deity for the concordance between symbol and thing, between language and things

**

can someone else besides me feel <u>this</u> pain?
is the language in which we express our feelings private?
am i writing in a private language?

></br>the swans, they're not here
> it's too hot for them

the body starts to generate heat. felt, i'm wrapped in it, in the snow,

between these two phrases
- i) (such names, like Persian cities: Susa, Persepolis) the image of an indigent hiding in a packaging plant
- ii) i don't want to extend the sequence: Boys-shaman-snow: i make myself recall photograms of French soldiers still upright, it snows
immediately "German soldiers"
i repress "German soldiers," the pity i feel for these German soldiers fallen in the snow, make myself go back to the retreat of Napoleonic forces

(narratives: the idea of progress and the centrality of man-reason as motor of those great narratives)
- a) ....
- b) on a distant level: fascism

this idea, set off in parentheses and quotations, then a (which i don't write down) and b which emerges at the least spark of contact
i try to get interested in the question, it's not interesting. The bread is raw

thinking of that word "zebra"

is like believing the earth is still a flat disk

★★

there are various trees, fallen, and the mountain stays up, unstuck, because it leans on the wall of the room in which i write
the forest takes up one of the four corners of my table, the corner where the sun rises

on the summit a bear ambles in the snow (a bear mannequin)

between me and the forest, diagonally: framed photographs
a gasoline heart, a purple plume, a stork, Snow White's slipper
and then the forest

i know it'll hurt to clean out the forest

she speaks of his body as if it had nothing to do with her, she'd speak of her own the same way; she speaks of bodies as if of nature

bodies have names, she constructs phrases that start with the name

bodies, the names those bodies utter, are compact, prior even to the concept "organic"; she situates herself in front of them by means of oral transmission, like someone who says
– the mountain was razed by enemy tanks

bodies, names, such and as she speaks, belong to the destruction and bodily resurrection of the dead
– go forth, multiply yourselves

(nothing common exists in language)

she doesn't really understand **anything she reads, forces herself** (50 daily fragments, 500 every 10 days), keeps reading. It is a writing exercise

this reading, without full understanding, removes her from the world, from any concern except advancing in her trajectories of reading
it is a breathing exercise

she finds calm in writing

anticorrosive, the vanished girl who was me in the forest exerts a kind of control over my writing desk the pain does not stop and all the scarlet symbols are with Jivi Noor

    she left the house early and got her ticket early

what did they talk about?

about a satellite that in some past decade centralized all information from european agencies and wasn't profitable in his view as half the news was sold to asian countries

near the end of the trip he (her seatmate) asked if she was interested in what he'd said
to which she (Jivi Noor) answered that nothing he'd told her was of the least interest but that from the moment they'd met, she'd been drawn by his voice and it was this she had listened to and nothing else

        bus depot (the ticket collector issues Jivi Noor a ticket and advises
        "she could take that bus but would have to tell the driver her ticket had been issued much earlier than she'd arrived – one way of seeing the world a little – though that bus isn't even scheduled to stop in the station we're in")

    m.o. seated in the bus placidly dozing

    restaurant in the author's native city

    coffee shop where possibly

                (a particularly hard winter)

it consists (beauty) of a forest, soon the vegetation thins out and a little further, a meadow. In the open, a spiral architecture of transparent walls (invisible to the eyes); in the entrance, a dead body; in the centre or chamber, a man who explores this archeology, labyrinth or ruin.
It happens on Venus, a planet

we'd already seen through the flower-mirrors (LSD trips), lysergic yew furniture

with time, the remains of the tomb (where the girl lies) were moved to the family crypt "thus i was deprived of a spatial intimacy in contemplation" Jivi Noor thought, "in literary sepulchres, transported by the tempest". So vegetation covered the transparent walls of the building
"and archaic diction acquired suddenly, so remote are the coffins i inhabit". They're not a dream, nor madness "the strange amphitheatre of Jekyll, the writing cabinets"

the tombstones toppled over. But i don't stay long in the caverns "what's so poetic in profaning graves, in trying to revive the dead?" even though *this room full of catalogued inert limbs, its floor sticky and full of blood and bits of human remains...* (all the sojourns of Writing) vaguely Jivi Noor it's the Nile and it's Cleopatra (Elizabeth Taylor) and it's sublime, but the palm grove and small wooden pier are surrounded by alders, pale as dead children, and oaks. But it's the Nile and she imagines the tidal pools and fertile muck, and the dawn of writing and cultivation. Perhaps they too were tired of oases. And she imagines temples. But this river is a river of fast rapids, one of the rivers of a nation remote, roiling

because that swan shouldn't have been there, in the pool, beside a remnant of dock and huge stones. It's when something shouldn't be there but appears, as a god might have in ancient Greece, pearls in the mouth (not your teeth, pearls). Pearls, in the mouth

coral on the lips; you have to see it, a fan of coral, latticed on the lips

but her lips were magnificent
you'd almost say they were coral
(to the point of drawing blood)

this journey might have happened at any lost point in the youth of Mariana (any woman today aged between 40 and 55). Night, lying on the blue train seat, head against the window, she contemplates *the grandiose Canadian landscape of lakes – which a light wind ripples – and interminable birch forests.* Preference for noctural-moving panoramas. London, at dawn, uve K. enters the clinic, M heads for the British, later the Tate: Rothko, Naum Gabo, Pevsner. The bison of Nevada interrupt the journey

the same thing all over (with mosquitoes)

now you're in what may be a perfect parallelepiped with stairs to the roof and two italianate alcoves communicating with twin tunnels of white fog (coral fossilized and smelling intensely of sulphur). There's writing on all the walls. The bartender, an old cupid with quiver and arrows, sets a stone cup on the table. You don't drink, you memorize the countersigns of poems (celtic warriors, baked into corn bread). In instantaneous mutation, you enter, stand up, fade out

what fascinated me about the radio was its keyboard (elephant ivory) and the greenlit mermaid eyes of a glide that regulated the volume; i was mesmerized and pretended it was me making that music (i made as if playing the piano) soaring over the savannah, with two hundred thousand elephants, from the jungle

truly (uve K.)

hot objects, of writing

– what matters is loss, all the times you pulled through.
   Benjamin explains it well
– i thought that was Mallarmé
– Mallarmé was metaphor, reasoning is from Benjamin
– and if you win?
– it's repoker
– and if you win again?
– then... you have to change game or... change tables

think of cities, **where merchandise plops in the purple mud of the tropics**

out of some verdescent churchyard, lost between massive atlantic shields (Jivi Noor) where the rockface, sea-battered, alters landscape in an extreme allegory
nor from its precipitation, untransferable

but the novelist wants to get a plot going, lead the characters someplace, a hotel ("you're everything i abandoned, the inferno before a plate of grapes, in Heraklion"), a ship

she loves a dorsal antarctica, so much she can't go forward, she only does so out of impossible measurement and progress, incalculable time or a transparent barrier, of beauty

with unrelenting attentiveness:
– that's why she describes the forest?

(the peoples under the tent are flickers in the inexorable wandering of phantoms)

and the walls of Jericho tumble

where music must be interpreted as spirit of abundance

just as the raised banner for a brief instant is lifted higher by the gust of gasoline only to fall again, carbonized, into the centre of the void or stone we were protecting

"study for a murder": the lovers are encircled, the majolican urns crumble, are served up in salad

(Percy Bysshe Shelley: some of his characters decide to lend their voices to this "ship without dryads")

DEMOGORGON: did you hear that? what's up with this woman! she's reduced romantic-sublime poetry to a repertoire of commands and then claims corporations are the paradigm of word contests
SPIRIT OF ASIA: she talks of building a bridge, from the cataclysms to someplace, a village that doesn't exist, that only the poem imagines, a dystopia
DEMOGORGON: but the "poets" (paradisiacal a-graphical ones, naturals) keep creating such beautiful poems
MULTITUDINOUS PROMETHEA: the monstrosity of being doesn't shatter them, the beauty of being, in the body, in words
NYMPH-ION: she doesn't talk of "creation", nor of self-prostration before a simply overblown Nature, before a simply infinite number, nor of the anguish in suspecting that the imagination can't make the leap
DEMOGORGON: and the unions? their leaders claim the workers' movement no longer exists and that the politics of the state and the workers' struggle are the same
SPIRIT OF ASIA: unions, most of them, are corporations, televisual tournaments
DEMOGORGON: we could dig underground tunnels
NYMPH-ION: she knows more than this, knows she has to drive Surface Transport

CLOTHO: Orpheus... was he a poet?
LACHESIS: yes, but he didn't know how to write, he was an oral poet

    (paradise, that place for a-graphical poets)

are you madam a person who writes for other people?
- no, i'm not a person who writes for other people
- so, then, who do you write for?
- i write because language imposes itself on me
- as it does on others?
- not as it does on all others, many others don't produce language
- this obligation, is it a means of parturition?
- no, it can simply be gallantry
- it presents itself to you as an act of love?
- more as a passion, as a building might offer itself, a moral act, an ache, a pain
- is its fondness returned?
- insofar as my talent permits
- you write, then, for everyone
- for everyone, no, for some, for those who decide to accompany me on the adventure
- but exactly how does your affability win out?
- the same way the Duke of Nemours prevailed before his love, that is, with persistence: the most violent, least natural and steeliest in the world

prophecy is a mode of political organization
revelation is not operative

we were travelling **toward an outer space we didn't recognize and by slim chance found the way back; even then we were asking ourselves what weight, what thickness, what rhythm, what cadence**
through the texture of the first words written on leaves of the trees in paradise

— rosy balcony?
— dawn
— turquoised curtain?
— wave
— glass snake?
— stream
— antarctic stars?
— heart
— Bengali woman of the Ganges?
— celestial body
— woven snow?
— tablecloths
— purple lividity?
— [...]
— marbled transparencies?
— {...}
— intuitive gold?
— ?

Indian, fable, eastern sea: no paradisiacal language (no one was speaking) precedes the arbitrary word that elects itself as genesis

although Mariana, surrounded as she was by all kinds of people – farmwomen – while waiting in what was once the visitors' area of the city prison, was able to conceive of a certain Edenic condition. She knew they all bore a name and that by rare historical chance this name fit with the ancient legal concept of *natio*. She felt the weight of wings, curled her body in the red velvet chair and let her thoughts give way to melancholy – melancholy leads to discouragement yes but also to sure and serene contemplation or *drift across waters*. She thought about Benjamin and catastrophe theory, about the current state of language subject to the law of supply and demand like any merchandise, about Baudelairean shock and how by superimposing the scientific theory of cataclysms onto this shock it was possible to enter into a litigation, into the possible demands of irrationality –i, communist, don't speak for you, communists–. Given that under current communication conditions, experiences of language can't be had and, as a result, accession to a catalogue of memories is not feasible, it is only through phantasms or regulatory disasters that the muse is possible. Thus the age of beauty would be one interwoven with the figurations of a game; with a time, that of the game, which deliberately ignores any settled position

although Mariana was able to conceive of a certain Edenic condition even for naming, she was no bearer of the ancient Roman concept of law, in no way was she trying or intending to recuperate the old aura of words but rather

she was interested in the unsayable (in the nation, in the poem, in the union), in conflicts of incomplete information, in fractals, in linking a discontinuous and non-rectifiable grammar that produces not consensus but the unknown, the unexpected: these norms or fluids constitute the so-called eruptive or volcano theory; Empedocles, Empedocles!

Mariana obeyed, entered the former cell which once held up to 40 prisoners during the 3-year war badly designated as civil, today housing two state bureaucrats; she let the agent ink her finger and press marks on paper for renewal of the ID card that would deny her not only the aura from which she had already been expelled and that she thus did or didn't bear, but also her belonging to the political concept of nation as Mariana knew it, as the ability to make political decisions about her true nationality.
Mariana gathered compass, book and legend – the numbers totalled 34 in any direction – and went out into the commonality. Utopia the greyhound – a symbolic dog – leapt incessantly at her feet, scattering players, prescriptions, republic of the ideal future

----

(adapt your aspirations to our ends or we'll remove you from the game, Mariana heard the agent say)

the nation thus declaims the insufficiency of its knowledge, portrays itself without attributes
diaries, agendas: all vanish

those asleep and the bard who sleeps with them and murmurs in their dreams: Maximiliana took her heart from her chest and checked that it was a literate viscera

(Maximiliana Marie Isidore spoke out in the ancient high rainforest, while all the world's birds capped in celestial blue velvet wee heads fringed in charleston bangs were calling
Brothers! Galician brothers!
Satan, sorrow
and an intense smell of tricolour forest permeated the air)

Maxi recalled phone calls with the Directorate of Thought *18th of Floreal, the snow settles on the icy fountain,* ordered rum with a twist of pineapple

----

This region declares itself an autonomous or sovereign State, and adopts the democratic-republican form of government
Sovereignty resides in the totality of the Galician people. The universality of citizens active and domiciled in the territory of Galicia constitutes a political body permanent in character, that exercises its functions directly by universal suffrage and indirectly through authorities or powers established by the Constitution
All these powers act to represent the people; all are elective, removeable and responsible, and all recognize that their power is limited by the natural, unlegislatable and unprescribable rights of man and the citizen.

and other such echoes, a thousand dark solitudes, daring hieroglyphics, enigmas and lulled harps

----

(in the sanitorium washroom, a clear space) a group of actors sip tea
delight themselves with the coffin work on the tray: *the cups resemble funerary urns and the napkins shrouds*
INMATE *(he)* #1 – it seems she'd rinsed them – my curls– / and with gold she tied them
INMATE *(she)* #2 – my brother turns on the device – a cathodic vitrine – , eats there, sups there; doesn't rise from his chair all day – three, four A.M. – eighty pills

We, working men and women of Galicia, together in Vigo under the most adverse circumstances our class has recently known, wish to take the floor to proclaim...

INMATE *(he)* #3 – i'm in a rush, i know, it's suffocating to recount this soap opera
seeds came out of me, my period came at the wrong time, i lost half a stone, spent a fortune on underwear, new swimsuits, shoes. On Saturday, Fernando'd stayed with a friend to go to the chalet, i was officially supposed to go with Teresa to watch Holy Sunday videos. i get on the plane soaked in sweat, after endless waiting

MAXI – when the party's over, the muse runneth over, enters the dream of men
chews cellophane, pale viscera of Dionysus
this is politics sampled
cold

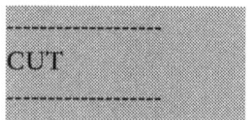

cut the roses, make a
bouquet
bestow it on me

sovereignty lies in the ever-so christian countryfolk of Galicia and in the vines, those brides of mystery in fog that breaks darkly into tears, into fogbanks even darker, into the strong walls raised by giants; into our hearts, lily and golden glass

and my beloved came and opened the iron-clad trunk
and started to pull out snowballs wrapped in coloured cloths

---

sanatorium washroom; the inmates still at the tea party, amuse themselves watching snow toys

---

and the first was Don Alvaro dressed as Peter Pan or blackbird pecking catalan grapes
INMATE #1 — there was another one we really liked: *of suave, fine velvet/the ship comes in mourning//long chains of roses/and black swans*
in the lapping of waves/ that escort it in circles, formed from mystery
and it was a ball of music
INMATE #2 — another we'll show you was Dona Rosalia, tiny as Anglor; she was happy and naked, wrapped in a florentine green parasol
and with a golden beltlet
to the back of her knee
INMATE #1 — and we saw the ball of Paris with no metro and streets full of people holding signs showing their destination, and there was no Paris metro because of a transit strike, the workers were that strong and we knew the Seine flowed shoeless
CHARLOTTE CORDAY — in the manor garden at a tiny patio table, there was Otero, a waltz was playing, it was the famed

cabaret *A Bilbaína* and with Nordic grief he wrote "as a child my father hunted buffalo on horseback. Long live free Warsaw!"
CHORUS OF BLACKMARKETEERS — and finally the loving gardens of Fontainebleau-Satania where five poet queens born in the 70s (ERGA, assassination of S. Allende) spent days of leisure
so lovely!
COULMIER, sanatorium director — and we wait for this ball of string to unwind to the end

> Galicians, be deserving of living among the world's new democracies. [...] and may the only cry from your lips be the cry of great peoples: Freedom or death!

PIMENTEL FASHIONS, special prices for the dead

boots off the drowned -------------------- $5
green fisherman's suit, hands
resting on livid temples------------------ $5
crêpe bands for stars---------------------- $5
luminous ivories (for her)--------------- $5
cloying syrup--------------------------------- $4
shut-in shades------------------------------- same
trade almanacs
wreaths of lilies
jack-knives for dream terror
raw silk suit---------------------------- unknown
white shirt, black suit, shiny tie,
new shoes for a village burial
pins to poke in the eyes of birds
roses still budding
mirrors without memories...

        (discounts for selected poets
        who know how to pluck mute strings)

extracelestial murmur of the spheres:
humus

alright! don't get on my case, here come the Galician bagpipes
– cherubim, enter at dawn

----

chronology of practice, synopsis

        1829 — Nicomedes Pastor Díaz
                  A Alborada (1828)

        1863 — *Cantares Gallegos*

– are you, madam, saying that sovereignty resides in Literature?
– lyric doesn't think the world, but invents the names that declare
   the world

           Pondal
           Curros   Cabanillas (1876-1957)
           Rosalia   F. Herrera (1869-1950)
                                Viqueira (1886-1924)

Pondal (1835-1917)
Rosalia (1837-1885)   Wordsworth: *I wandered lonely as a cloud*
                                    (1789)
Curros (1855-1908)   Byron (1788)
                                                Baudelaire
                                                Rimbaud
Jules Verne (1829)

1863 — *Cantares Gallegos*   1880 — *Follas Novas*

"the invention of the names that declaim the world"
assumes a position: that the muses are determined under political conditions

        Pintos (1811-1876)
        Añón (1812- 1878)   Mallarmé (1848-1892)
                                   Nerval (1800-1855)
        Tsvetaeva (1892-1941)   Baudelaire (1821-1867)
        Akhmatova (1890-1966) Rimbaud (1854-1891)

                [more divine that the Citerea rose
                more gallant than glad springtime
                Venus a lover to me]

– what do you mean madam by foundational-political texts and narratological-historical texts?

Leopardi (1798-1837)

                            Trakl (1887-1914)
                            Martí (1798-1837)

(1840-50) there is a proletarian political capacity,
a political capacity for nation, *there's a teeming colony in the Court, and it will rise up from this humiliation and abasement (April 2, 1848)*

nowhere do Liberty's words coincide with its acts

Liberty is the first modern lyric enunciator
but not as contradiction or antithesis, rather as what could never be synthesized
captured or grabbed

the muses compose names for the disappearence of the state

> [i, galician, speak for you, galicians
> a disastrous evil is on the loose
> a belief in the totalizing and totalistic power of truth]

the muses are devoid of object or history, but interiorize the system of their conditions – their own blindspot – and the effects of this system
the lyre intervenes in reality and produces effects in itself; it acts outside itself — Immortal — because of what it produces in itself
it's a process capable of inventing the names of truth

i call to you masked knight of Reboraina (Otero Pedrayo)
to you the exiles in teeming London of 67 and to you Lady Eve – a frozen isle of madness in each eye –
and to you, Dominique Roturier: "To the glory of Daguerre and Laplace", republican, Limian and positivist
and to you copious wines and monophysites of Lebanon
– in Aden, you'll be able to see and love a true Mermaid, without repugnance: the tail rhythmically increases pleasure

amid the bustle and oriental voices in the port and streets of Singapore

the old pilot who'd brought emigrants by the hundreds from the port of Vigo to America recollects and describes:

(mairexa: fish of tricolour beauty)

how over the course of that war, bands of dozens of mairexas, schools of them, escorted his ship jammed with men and women loyal to Galicia and loyal to the Republic

Rafa Villar (Cee, 1968-   )

there is Lyric: there is no suture

> it's not that *it's not possible to say,* nor even a
> limit of *no, it's not possible for language.* My
> radical resemblance to the animal,
> to the star

solar matter that frees me
   that sets me loose

LEGACY

so any foundational-political text (foundational does not mean a text about origin) of feminine authorship is immediately ma-de into ma-le or whiskers that sprout from him and have to sprout from Rosalía

equinox: the poem fabricates itself completely de-naturalized as sign, context and time
   Defines itself as construction of a determinate species in a changing world
   As object of knowledge it's a generative, corporeal and semiotic nodule

in no way essence *(verbum divinum)*	codes
or *natural* origin or home	dispersion and creation of networks
(house) of language	fragmentation
	GENOME

> **Trip: Itinerary**
>
> **from a "comfortable" organic-essentialist society to a polymorphous information system (current violations)
> **essentialism: "ratio" (poem) centred in a unidirectional subject
> **representationism: the stability of the signified taken as a given
> **Linguistics: Claude Shannon for the Bell Telephone Company
> **context as artefact
> **the organic as human construction (post-biology)
> **simulacrum: copy or replica with no possible original
> **subject//poem: unstable, antiauthoritarian, fluid, continually changeable, but not relativist. Must cross borders, triumphing over them while it sites itself in its own corporeal and semiotic markers (nation, gender, race, desire or sexual preference, class, age...) and affirms its multiplicity
> METAPOETICS, for more information consult this author's other works in prose

a poem, successful replicant, is that which manages to persist
under copies of other poetic texts, over extended time,
measured in literary generations, and manages to propagate
many copies of itself

disassembled and	AND I ASSEMBLE IT AGAIN
a logic	DISTINCT FROM ORIGIN, FROM
	REPRESSION // NON OEDIPAL
near to	IDENTITY, LEGACY.

but if this artificial intelligence can thrive and grow on its own, human thought for the first time will live free of flesh and bone, according this mental offspring an earthly immortality that we ourselves are denied

GNOSIS

(after the mythical or technical narratives about origin)

woman, constellation, animal, cyborg

origin constructs itself auto-selects.

we take on the question, we murmuring ones – *with pallid chests* –
pneuma of spring

galician women are of honey poured [1]

CHORUS OF WOMEN WHO CROSSED THE ATLANTIC – our gaze is glassy so vitrified it would be cruel without the vegetal tenderness that warms our flesh; and under the honey, our steely nervation stratifies mountains
ROBERTO ARLT– although my body's blocked by the Galician landscape, my thoughts unravel in Buenos Aires, together with all Galicians, with all the Galician women who crossed the ocean, and i tell myself:
of stone the fountains, of stone the stakes that hold the vines, of stone the garden walls, of stone the bridges and roads that wind through corn, and of stone the poles that bear the wires, of oceanic stone. i think of Galician women who crossed the high seas
galician women are of honey poured
GIRL WHO CROSSED THE OCEAN – will we eat ice cream and moka in the garden of the Könisberg lovergirl? our grandparents, were they all in the vanguard?
LOVERGIRL OF KÖNIGSBERG – in this garden i grow white roses and ultrametaphysical carnations, my roses and carnations are "Pure Reason"; the author wanted this, that my love transform itself
GIRL... – our great-grandparents, were they in the vanguard too?

---

[1] — Arlt, son of Carolina Iobstraibitzer, so sensitive and fantasizing, and of Roberto Godofredo Christophersen, humble immigrant: Aguafuertes Gallegas, Ameghino Escritora S.A., Córdoba 1411, Rosario – Argentina

CHORUS OF GALICIAN WOMEN... –our grandparents were in the vanguard, our great-grandparents no, for them Galicia was a fact created by intelligence and driven by imagination, for them Galicia was an Ideal
GIRL – is it true we only exist in the pages of a book?
CHORUS... – we were a travelling race, aching with homesickness and ever rooted in our native soil. Waiting for snow to fall, petals of elderflower, such snow

> *from this crowd of Galician women came natural poetesses, with no need of poetic art, of musical art, or of the chant of organs. They create their own songs, invent tones and perform the chant, which is very singular and suave... [...]*

> **Galician mothers. So that your sons will die no more on foreign soil, so that you may blossom like spring in our homes instead of slaving on field and shore. Vote for the Galicianist Party slate**

Lady Angelina of the far cove, Marquise of Floravia, takes hold of the dagger... Then considers a flask of poison. Then slowly caresses the handle of a long saddle pistol... sanatorium bells ring out backstage
Maximiliana rises to her full height

Comrades
we gather here again today to celebrate the Day of the Republic
i'd like to say that, effectively, the nation exists but there's something further that exists as well, beyond nation, and this beyond is called Independence
effectively capital exists
and a sole truth of capital: "anything goes as long as it makes a profit", the nub of modern nihilism
History withers, creating the illusion of an immovable present, perpetual
this conversion, announcement of the dusk of ideologies, has one goal: political asepsis
and its transformation into a management tool
the worst is that organizations (political and union) didn't flee from this entirely, though they once represented the horizon of emancipation
But this is how they built their consensus, structured on mercantile language

Yet we gathered here today are not profitable and do not accept the laws of political management
we don't cover up for the constitutive violence of capital
because exploitation exists
because class society exists

because History exists and so do principles, revolutionary truth and fidelity, fierce loyalty to the words of national and class emancipation

false consensus, the false ethics of human rights, false equalities and differences between women and men, the alienating fragmentation of the subject... are all ideas of the bourgeoisie and serve it only
they impose behaviours on us and above all values
they are natural dominators
and turn us into the vanquished, before or without a struggle

politics begins when a class utters the names of revolutionary practice
communism is not an Ideal, it is a praxis that annuls and surpasses productive and ideological alienation
revolution is the right to liberty, to national sovereignty
this "cry of nature" (Kant), this "inundation" that overwhelms the dikes (Fichte)

the "right to revolution" (Staatsveränderung) is as crucial as liberty
republic or democracy, these two words, synonyms

we, men and women, the workers of Galicia...

★★
★★

the piano is open... a sheet of white paper rests on the stand. Don Guido is an elderly gentleman very refined and courteous (Don Guido speaks)

> the wind is the baroque function of clouds, or route of all news from circle to polar circle
> – this wind was educated in the parks of Vienna

from the iceberg-sculpture cloud
from an air-cupola, in a trice it turns the sea into a
hemispherical Versailles
it marries well with sky, marries well with sea
in anyone's mind, a philosophy is born, Leibnitz or ionic
while thousands of king's cups of Thule float or sink into
the sea
the coordinates shimmer too (throwback to a child toying with the sphere, or mapamundi, how it could be confused with a big pumpkin in the field of turnip greens after the corn harvest, or in the yard where flagstones glisten ever outward in Mercator projection) at the seaside we played, pretending we could see the latitudes, every five degrees they curved out of gurgling foam

we might have rowed over the ruins of Atlantis
you feel it in your guts: the presence of African birds
the period of the mass emigation of the eels
the state of the diastole of the Atlantic heart of warmest
waters
the last known coordinates of wrecked ships
the prediction of the last dip of the polar star

(Don Guido is decked out in the grand old style... Bit by bit, Lady Angelina forgets the phosphoric light. Bells are still ringing backstage) [1]

★★★★★★★★★★★★★★★★★★★★★★★★★★★★★★★★★★★★
★★

---

[1] *The Prior's Dismay, and Others (O desengano do prioiro e outros)*, Otero Pedrayo, 1952

HÖLDERLIN – "at the extreme limit of distress, there is in fact nothing left but the conditions of time and space"
ANTIGONE – that's my condition exactly...

*

    psychological description of the muse or Island, desolation: colony/*created on the order of Zeus in the armchair, we see the muse vanish in a thick cloud of dust that completely covers her: she's off to collect a legacy*

Present:
Maria
Chimera Drake
Frenchwoman
heroine lost from a galactic war or wee field birds
Eugene, muse
Xoán Carlos Rodríguez (this poem is for him, for Xoán Carlos Rodríguez)
Others, male and female...

MARIA – the present conspires because it begs to be written; you say i have to find a pet for the muse, a capuchin monkey...
MUSE – i was born right in the middle of the Cold War yet don't remember Korea; the 50s were a decade of manifest sickness; in the 70s we went into the world

> at this point the reader can go reread Pushkin, and find in the stanzas of Onegin a detailed and excellent description of the muse; lines like *not only did he witness sadness and disappointment but also a youth prematurely gone to seed; at the same time, he flashed a ring of jet carved with a skull*
> The reader has his own tastes, i realize; they are or should be different than mine

then the muse discusses how to escape the Bluebeard's-castle-library-bookstore, as she dialogues with a heroine lost from a galactic war

voice, who knows whose – hell is perfect and works
heroine lost from a galactic war – but what are you saying, are you saying that my party's name is in the Book of Usurpations or usurpers?
Eugene, muse romantic and not-so – i tell you i read it there, the symbols of your party, there they were, where it was explained as well that evil is an effect of good because at first this Union was well founded but that after the crisis of 75 or somesuch, nothing was left, a sect, nothing, the best were expelled or left, anyone can read it; may the force be with you! i'm in a hurry

> (not so much in the symbols – Book of Usurpations – but in the idea and alliance, the bad conscience that you were part of the origin, not that of the moneyed minority but of the poorer strata, dispossessed of nation)

> *my recklessness, terrible greenery. Ask me to lie down in the dust, maybe, so that maybe*
>   *i can continue you (Xohana Torres)*

**

        they go into the garden, a playing card
pull out the suckers, their eyes are already green starlets of yew

tale of the girl who lives in a yew who sleeps in its slow and curved roots in the embrace of the great mother polar Bear. And every morning, she shatters, with her wee feet, puddles of ice so as to go to school
wooden shoe, *sabot* heart – girls who leap and dance
little clog
SABOTAGE

the playwright, with garden equidistant
writes
interminable dialogues between Chimera Drake and Maria
incessant discussion, so many impassioned words, frank debate:
about national Identity and the rural classes
Without shattering in the least the fullness and solidarity of their political convictions

MARIA — we held our meetings after dark, with people around the speaker to mask whose voice it was. Before the crisis of 75 and before the police shot Moncho Reboiras

a coffee shop trotskyist lights the stage

fuchsia, wisteria
bougainvillea

***

   repertoire of Russian phrases to characterize a romantic-anarchic and, in the end, nationalist muse; authors abandoned or death-longing, but it was a lie

   44=4+4=8+1999=1674=1+6+7+4=1+8=9=6, hexagon
   44=4+4=8+1666=2007=2+0+0+7=9=6, hexagon

   or cellular condition of the honey that nourished Pindar
   under the mouth's sky
   underground tomb of the viceroy

all around you, like weak maritime lightning
and the encounter at the white coral atoll and a viceroy gone mad

it was how Eugene imagined the resurrection
that emblem the poet keeps in her heart; the muse refuses
the reproduction of its face
constructs a sky with rowboat splinters
on any seaside promenade:
summer tourists

certain anchylosed or unreal ideas of the muse, his adoration by Emma Bovary
his opinions on the labour market and the work of women
the passion for crime as mathematical mechanism
the paternity of the muse, the absence of hope
Chimera will explain that without hope, the revolution is not possible
the clandestinity and physical mysteries of Eugene
the confusion between literature and truth
his physical and mental aging, the detention of time

(Chimera and Maria dance on the mountainside, pursued by the heroine of galaxies and wee field birds who controls the coffee shops in the port)

they duck into an 80s bar

someone should really attend to the Basic Aspects of the syntax of my writing --
----

performers:

muse – (not to be confused with the one in the previous poem)
soul – daydreaming, not paying the slightest attention to what anyone says

★★★★★★★

Dialogue between this Muse and the Soul

MUSE – come close, good woman, i'll explain the difference between the beautiful and the sublime
for the first, a kind of common sense has to be attuned – it's a distinterested pleasure – so that sensibility and the faculty of rational organization can find a path of open harmony, and it has to be immediately operative
this pleasure is promise of happiness, the promise of a community of feeling between the subject in and of herself and alongside others

in the sublime[1] we abandon the idea of a community of *sensus comunis*, which is to say, of an instantly communicable *sentimentality*
the poem can then be the incalculable *"faint tugging"*
(– this disaster of the imagination, the cause of the sublime – can be seen as an indication that forms, verse, free association of images, rhythm, rhyme, are no longer relevant under its sign)

---

[1] As far back as the seventeenth and eighteenth centuries, this name was used – by Boileau in his well-known translation of Lonxino – and classic poetics drew to a close; romanticism triumphed, which is to say, modernity.

thus when Dedalus utters his famed phrase and Antigone answers
i hear the ruin of all <u>space</u>, shattered glass and toppling masonry, and <u>time</u> one livid final flame
with the underlined words, god withdraws and nothing more happens to the hero, there's no destiny for him; nature – domus, heroine – is lacking

for such a terror (Burke) – that by which nothing comes to pass – to be suffused with pleasure, the fear it elicits must be held in suspense (so that the soul might thus be free of threat, by being deprived of light, language, life...) and we wouldn't call it pleasure but delight

thanks to this, the soul welcomes the agitation between life and death. In this way, the poem now freed of all imitation of what is not – nature – becomes artefact, simulacrum, and presents the unpresentable in language in an entirely new phrase

in this "here and now" the will unravels
the poem destroys the spirit's presumption of mastery over time
the feeling of the sublime is the name of these "mortal remains"

to be exact, the feeling of the sublime appears when representation of free forms is lacking; it is however compatible with the unformed
to be exact, it appears when the imagination that presents form falls short and it has then to arrive through the mediation not of a god but of an Idea of reason which is the Idea of liberty

from this point, the poem proclaims nothing; and we perceive it as being closer to ethics (liberty) than to aesthetics (common taste)

the word has the force of an obligation toward a second person: LISTENTOME
nothing is told in the poem (the intrigues of the spirit are already undone)
it is in itself a purely visual, intellectual and auditory event

****

MUSE — (continues his speech...)
thus this type of poem isn't regulated by taste (without prince, people, god, without nature, without hero, without heroine...) what is the poem?
(do something cultural! be mercantile! make money!)
inscribed in the poem is the email of the first lady
we'll answer her every request

THROUGH THE SUBLIME, Antigone responds

But the rewriting contends as much with the beautiful as with the sublime; this opens the door to the RELATION BETWEEN ETHICS AND AESTHETICS

this rewriting that turns the clock back to zero

matter, poetic matter, doesn't wait for destiny, awaits nothing, doesn't call the spirit
offers itself to neither dialogue nor dialectic
words speak, whistle, pluck ... ever prior to the poem, and always say something other than what the poem means and what the author wants to signify in giving it form. WORDS DESIRE NOTHING (despite the spirit's presumption of mastery over time). They are non-desire, the meaninglessness of the poem, its multitude
this matter returns time and again, this matter, the soul
such ruins are the poem's subterranean manoeuvres, the staging and action of the

powers
of language
that do not obey
the undescribable
in the face of destiny

HÖLDERLIN — "we are far from god (domus-nature), the galaxies of resonance flee at top speed from the templum sanctum–where the first sound rang out. They sing, without a doubt, linking various frequencies, levels, durations. But the unparalleled, the unrepeatable, does not radiate from the linking. It obscures itself and offers itself, perhaps, in each sonic atom." [2]

****

ARENDT – "I still am thinking of Wystan, naturally, and of the misery of his life, and that I refused to take care of him when he came and asked for shelter. Homer said that the gods spin ruin to men that there might be song and remembrance. Helen said in the *Iliad*: Zeus brought evil on her and Paris *"so that in days to come we shall be a song for men yet to be* and Hecuba (in Euripedes), about to be carried off into slavery, says – consoles herself? – without this disaster *we would be unfamed, unsung, not something to be remembered by mortals in the future.*
Well, he – Auden, poet – was both the singer and the tale." [3]

---

[2] For this paragraph and, generally, for the entire poem, see: Jean-François Lyotard, *The Inhuman: Reflections on Time*, Cambridge: Polity Press, 1991.
The Hölderlin quote is fake, naturally, but not that of Dedalus, even though it doesn't exactly fit what follows it... I'd recommend going back a few pages, to the previous dialogue between H. and Antigone.
[3] *Between Friends: The Correspondence of Hannah Arendt and Mary McCarthy, 1949-1975*, NY: Harcourt Brace, 1995, p.343-4.

what more can a breast be but food and stormy sky? the cells of course do whatever they please

---

HERIBERTO – "...look how pretty the little town is, with its adored farmworker nabbed by the intellectual patriot, adolescents chaste and well brought up, from a family of storekeepers who wave forests of flags in the wind of the Mother Country, the whole lot yelling, possessed by purest ire, invincible anger and crushing fear of liberty."
COULMIER – (startled, prose) i can't let people go around saying such things. We are citizens of a new era... artisans of change and growth. Thus...
MME COULMIER – this is subversion. This is intolerable
WOMAN INTERNEE – (plays the role of Roux)
  but the Revolution lasts but an instant like lightning
  that falls as light
  astonishing

(the nurses hit the internees and knock them down; the sweet sisters of charity pray in the face of disorder)

CHORUS OF INTERNEES – (singing Weiss's song)
    Charenton, Charenton
    Galicia nation
    Galicia nation
    Revolution, Copulation
    Revolution, Copulation

            Tempest

they glow pale-white and cold, the snow's blossoms and concept of camelias
five hundred eyes for Hera

with no real problem other than a stormy sky looming inside her; the cells, of course, do whatever they please
ambiance.

galicia: symphonic **poem; my trust is indissoluble**

Liberty Aguirre's literary identity card (DNA spiral)

generation of the *Festas Minervais* – no blood relationship
mother – marriage promoter
father – generation of 1936 (dead)
grandfathers – in the vanguard
grandmothers – illiterate

★★

a philosopher visits Charenton: speech to all present

PEPA LOBA – (romping through Sade)
what a beautiful death! so well-written! Madame Clariña de Saint-Vaats with her feather boa. All the nightingales and skinny turtledoves fly into her hands. "the anti-slavery rebellions: a spectre runs all through the old asiatic mode of production

the rain pours into the cells, the internees in chorus get set to write the "song of the imprisoned lover" [1]

how can we tell if the waters are enamored or not?

remains of grape pomace and parasol mushrooms that are stork-white inside or pink like angel hair or new celtic oak

---

[1] TRANSLATOR'S NOTE: "cantiga do amante preso" – written in prison by Mendéz Ferrín in 1969 and published under the pseudonym Heriberto Bens when MF was not allowed to publish . . . *cantigas* are medieval poems.

a splash of sun when they open on the hearthstone, a smoky gold
we eat this, this flower

my work deals with the
language of origin or the language of lost origin
territory or absence of territory
history or the possible construction of history
identity or an impossible identity
class structure and class segments
the conscious and the unconsious
desire and the prolongation of ecstasy
profit
plus-value and silence
the box-in-valise Museum of Marcel Duchamp
(including "The Large Glass")
turkish restaurants
the court of human rights
the sculpture of Naum Gabo and Antoine Pevsner
panic
culture

"A *nation* has at least nine aspects: professional, administrative, state, class, geographical, sexual, conscious, unconscious and perhaps yet another that is intimate; it unites all of them in itself but they do not cohere; the *nation* is but a vessel washed by all these streams that converge in it."

Robert Musil. A *Nation* Without Qualities (1952)
(quote substantially altered by the author)

RESIDENTS OF THE PHRENOPATHIC ASYLUM VISIT LIBERTY AGUIRRE IN HER CURRENT HOME

(today) we're eating lunch in Eigelstein

against the state of origin
having come through immaterial damage and the loss of my nation (Galicia)

we spin three hundred sixty degrees above the Rhine,
which our women ancestors crossed at Easter in the year 406 in their sleighs and frost
toward gallaecian LANDS

the poem, like the city, destroyed and built again
and, here and there, remains of history

biological remains
bodies, carried off,
over the implacable digital surface

in the retina, nearly sinking under the weight of coal, barges

capital produces insecurity
its profit, the refusal to invest in social technology
produces our inability to live
produces panic

        (i don't recognize the legitimacy of my acts)

so my nightmares get mixed up with the dream of trees, in Germany

let there be vegetation, fluids, air for this poem i abandon mortal
and *physis*

she loves

Acknowledgements

The publishers thank the Xunta de Galicia (the Regional Government of Galicia) for their financial assistance, without which this publication would not have been possible.

Some of these poems have been previously published or accepted for publication in English by: *VeRT* #8 (USA, 2003); *Jacket* #28 (Australia, 2005); *RESPIRO* (Argentina, 2005); *1913: A Journal of Forms* (USA, 2005); *Fourteen Hills Review* (USA, 2006); *NO: A Journal for the Arts* (USA, 2006); *The Capilano Review* (Canada, 2006); *Shearsman* (UK, 2006).

Chus Pato (María Xesús Pato Díaz) was born in 1955 in Ourense, Galicia (north-west Spain). All of her work is written in Galician, a language which is closely related to both Spanish and Portuguese.

She teaches History and Geography at a high school in the interior of Galicia. In her words: "writing metabolizes the world, even that world that cannot be absorbed into writing." And: "I have a predilection for those constructions which investigate the possibility of a language-thinking that refuses to repeat the already-written and lives in contact-lamination with the seams of the unsayable, of what hasn't yet been written into the corporeality of the poem." "To me, the poem is a freedom-machine." "My autobiography? It does not always seem to be mine; sometimes I would rather have other lives. Insofar as all autobiography participates in fiction, I prefer not to be forced to choose, so I opt not to have one."

Her work: *Urania* (Calpurnia, Ourense, 1991), *Heloísa* (Espiral Maior, A Coruña, 1994), *Fascinio* (Toxosoutos, Santiago de Compostela, 1995) *Nínive*, (Xerais, Vigo, 1996), *A ponte das poldras* (Noitarenga, Santiago de Compostela, 1996), *m-Talá* (Xerais, Vigo, 2000), *Charenton* (Xerais, Vigo, 2003), and a selection translated into Spanish by Irís Cochón: *Un Ganges de palabras* (Puerta del Mar, Málaga, 2003). A selection from *m-Talá*, in Erín Moure's translation, has been published in Canada.

Politically engaged, Chus Pato is a member of PEN Galicia as well as *Redes escarlata*, a leftist cultural group that supports independence.

www.ingramcontent.com/pod-product-compliance
Lightning Source LLC
Chambersburg PA
CBHW031156160426
43193CB00008B/393